The Webinar Jumpstart Workbook

Actionable Steps for Scaling Your
Impact and Your Influence
In the Next 30 Days

Aprille Reed

THIS WORKBOOK BELONGS TO:

_____

_____

_____

Would you like a FREE 8.5 x 11 downloadable and fillable PDF version of this workbook?
Go to **www.aprillereed.com/bookresources/**

And how would you like a FREE mini workshop training exclusively for owners of this workbook to help you work through this workbook and get the most out of it?
Go to **www.aprillereed.com/bookresources/**

TABLE OF CONTENTS

TABLE OF CONTENTS

TABLE OF CONTENTS

Introduction

Congratulations on getting this webinar workbook. By doing so, it means you're ready to take your business to the next level. However, over the years, I have found that the main problem that gets in people's way is not knowing where to start. You can check that problem off the list now that you have this workbook.

But the next problem hides in the mental game. Your mental game can propel you to success or beat you down to your knees. And I had to adapt this most powerful mindset to drive myself to webinar success:

It's the fact that **EVERYONE has something they can teach.**

Maybe this isn't you. You already know what you would like to offer, but a lot of new and aspiring entrepreneurs tell me, "Webinars seem cool, and I'd love to do a webinar, but I don't have anything to teach."

Trust! If blood is going through your veins, you have something to teach. You don't have to be this so-called "Expert." A third-grader is an expert to a preschooler. All you have to do is be a few steps ahead.

The fact of the matter is that nobody is ever born knowing everything; we all have to learn something.

And it's because MOST people in your inner circle (friends, family, your audience) are not experts in your particular field, and they are STRUGGLING to accomplish what you already know how to do, and they need a guide.

They haven't a clue who to turn to for help. And so as the guide (aka expert), that's where you come in.

Have you ever seen the movie "Catch Me If You Can"?

Frank William Abagnale Jr., a con man, check forger, and imposter, played by Leonardo DiCaprio, consents his way into college and becomes a sociology professor. He was able to teach by always being one chapter ahead of his classes.

OK, don't take that the wrong way. Not telling you to con people, but what I'm saying is that we all have something we know how to do better than others, and we all have something we can teach.

If you are a parent, that fact alone, you are an expert of many hats. Even if you aren't, you have life experiences and knowledge that puts you ahead of the game.

 :: NEWS FLASH::

Your future customers and clients are not looking to become experts. All they want is to get the results that they want. And that's where you come in.

So don't believe that nonsense. You do have something valuable to teach, something worthwhile to share. You have to take action, go out there, and teach it.

And if you're looking for a platform that will get your voice heard to the masses, leverage your time while building your list, and your business, webinars by far are the way to go **(even if you don't know where to start).**

How To Use This Workbook!

This workbook is numbered as a countdown from day 30 down to day zero. Unlike traditional planners or workbooks that count up, this workbook counts down.

It is designed to **choose your webinar date early** on (**minimum 30 days from now**) and then counts down the days until you finally host your webinar and even what to do after the webinar.

When I decided to host my first webinar, it took me an entire year to create and launch it to the world. I had no goal and no deadline.

Once I finally set a date (30 days into the future) and told the world, I finally started working on my webinar daily. I had to finish it because people were signing up, so I had to do it or let them down.

Having that form of accountability while ticking off my calendar days kept things in perspective and moving forward.

You see, having a countdown will spring you into more action because you will know there are only 20 days until your webinar...10 days left until your webinar, and so on.

Use this workbook as a guide to help you stay on track and plan your next webinar.

Pre-Planning

Days 30 down to 28 are all about getting the preliminaries out of the way. You want your webinar to be profitable from the start, so you will decide on your lucrative niche and what you will sell during the first day. From there, start thinking about and gathering your webinar equipment. To help you with this list, go to page 107 of this workbook.

Week 1

Your first official week will count from **days 27 down to 21.** During this week, you will decide on your webinar topic and title. You'll also create the "What You're Going To Learn" bullets for your audience that you'll put in your emails and registration page. You will create graphics, get your webinar platform, start learning early on, and outline your webinar content.

Week 2

During this week, **days 20 down to 14**, we will get some necessary webinar pages out of the way. If you are brave enough, you can start sending traffic to your registration page in anticipation of your webinar. Yes, technically, your webinar isn't created yet, but what's a little deadline pressure to make sure you stay on task!!

Week 3

From **days 13 down to 7** is all about content and scheduling promo graphics on social media. His how to make the best out of your time, week two was about creating emails inviting your list to the webinar. You will use most of that same copy for your social media promos. I love to set it and forget it. Schedule what you can, but not all. People want to see you live, but to make it easier on you, schedule most of your posts.

Week 4

We're getting down to the nitty-gritty. You're going to love that you've scheduled your email broadcast and social media posts ahead of time. Week 4, **days six down to the day of the webinar,** is mostly about tying up loose ends and practicing, practicing, practicing your webinar presentation as if you were doing the real thing.

What The Tech?!

What equipment do you need besides a computer to present your webinar like a pro? Use this section as your tech guide.

Resources & Tools

Valued at $297, I just had to add this in. This section is devoted to the resources and tools you need to rock your webinars. One complaint I hear a lot is knowing the right resources to use for a webinar, taking weeks to sort out. (Not really, but analysis paralysis kicks in, and that is what takes weeks.) I hope that this resource section will help you save time and taking more immediate action.

PRE- PLANNING

COUNTDOWN FROM DAYS 30 To 28

Day 30
Lucrative Markets

It's planning day! You've decided to host a webinar (go you!), and your mind is racing for everything you need to do - I got you! Follow this planning day worksheet to breakdown what you need to figure out before inviting the world to your online event.

YOUR OFFER:

Whatever your offer entails, be sure that it falls into one of the **4 Mega markets.**

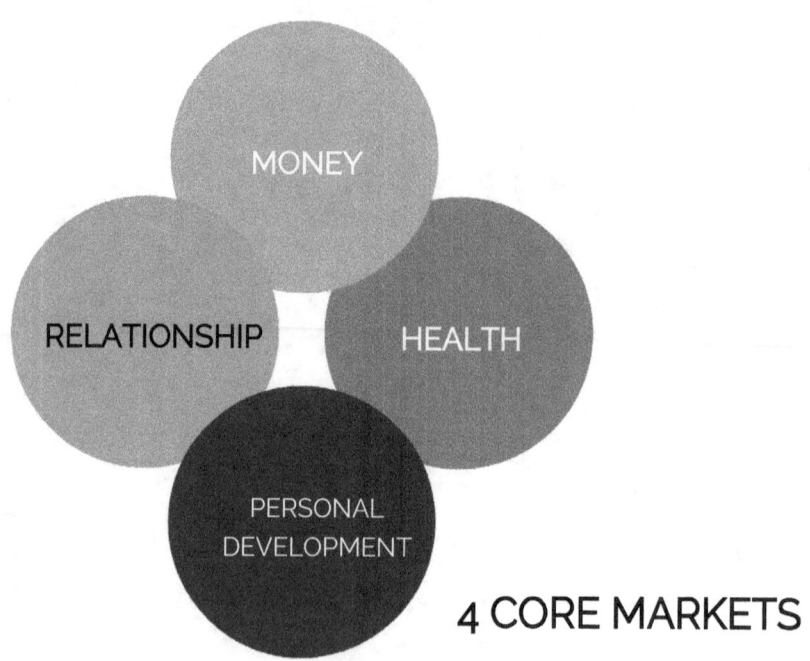

4 CORE MARKETS

CHECKLIST:

☐ Choose which market to place your product under.

☐ Decide on your offering and list it below.

Which mega niche does your offer fall under?

What will you be selling at the end of the webinar? This will impact your webinar topic and funnel, so choose wisely.

NOTES:

_____

_____

_____

_____

_____

_____

_____

_____

NOTES:

_____

_____

_____

_____

_____

_____

_____

_____

_____

_____

_____

_____

_____

Day 29
Planning Out Your Webinar

What time will you hold your webinar?

> !
>
> TIP: The best time, statistically, to host a webinar is 1:00 PM EST. This is going to depend on your audience and their location, however. If you work a 9-5 or if your audience includes people that work a corporate job, 1:00 pm EST is not going to be the best time. You may have to host your webinars in the evenings. Be mindful of dinner times, lunchtimes and weekends. Weekends are the least popular days for obvious reasons.

What webinar software will you be using?

Tech matters! Invest in a good microphone, and be sure you have excellent internet connectivity.

What email marketing system will you be using?

What landing page builder will you be using?

> **!**
>
> TIP: Your landing page MATTERS! You're going to need to choose a good landing page because this is how people are going to register for your Webinar. A successful landing page should have a story, a hook and WHY they need to sign up for your webinar. What sets you apart? Why are you the one they should learn from?

NOTES:

_____

_____

_____

_____

_____

_____

_____

NOTES:

_____

_____

_____

_____

_____

_____

_____

_____

_____

_____

_____

_____

_____

Day 28
Get Software and Schedule Your Webinar

It's getting real! Today, you will schedule your webinar in the software you will be using. The steps on this are going to depend on your webinar provider. I highly suggest you practice your platform early to get acquainted.

If using a free trial, you might want to wait a little closer to the webinar date but not too close. Give yourself plenty of time for any learning curve. See a list of webinar platforms on page 110.

EXERCISE

What software will you be using?

Have you scheduled your webinar?

☐ YES ☐ NO. If not, do so now.

NOTES:

_____

_____

_____

_____

WEEK 1

COUNTDOWN FROM DAYS 27 To 21

Day 27
Choosing Your Webinar Topic and Title

To promote your irresistible offer, you need to create a webinar topic and title that will engage and attract your audience!

Your offer and your topic need to be in total alignment, so there's no surprise that your topic will fall under the same mega niche category as your offer.

Your topic should fall under one of these categories:

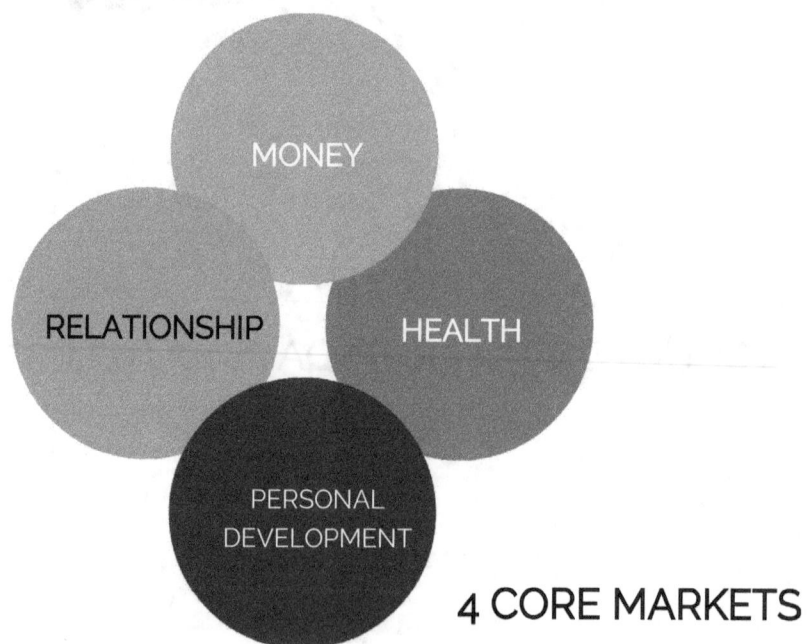

4 CORE MARKETS

You may be in a situation where you feel your topic doesn't fit into money, health, relationships, or personal development, so let's look at an example:

Your offer: Dog Training DVD video series. In particular, potty training your puppy.

But where does dog or puppy training fit? Personal development? Money? If you're unsure, you can choose to make the "marketing" fit any mega niche you want.

- **Money** - Potty training your puppy you save your from buying new carpet (here we are saving money)
- **Relationship** - Potty training your puppy will improve your relationship with your new puppy and ensure that you'll have a life companion. The #1 reason for people giving away their dogs is behavioral problems. Your spouse will appreciate it as well.
- **Health** - Potty training your puppy is sanitary for your children because who wants to crawl around dried urine in the house.
- **Personal Development** - Learning to care for and train a puppy will help you learn responsibilities and gear you for the real world.

Now that we have a topic: How To Potty Train, Your Puppy, it's time to create a title.

"How to" is the most common and best way to start a title if you are unsure. But now let's make it better:

Follow the script: How to (get the result) without (doing something your audience doesn't want) plus some numeric metric.

Here are some metric examples:

- In The Next 7 Days
- In The Next 30 Days
- The 7 Strategies To
- Top 10 Mistakes Most Creatives Do
- In Only 5 Minutes A Day
- In Little As 30 Minutes A Day

How To Potty Train Your Puppy In The Next Seven Days

Without Having An Accident.

BOOM!

Adding a metric (i.e., The Next Seven Days), you are building on the topic - and without having an accident, it makes it an irresistible title.

CHECKLIST:

☐ Choose what mega niche your topic will fall under. It should be the same as your offer.

☐ If your topic does not easily fall under one of the mega niches, decide how to market your topic to fit in only ONE mega niche category.

☐ Decide on your Topic and list it below.

☐ Using the script, create your webinar title and list it below.

EXERCISE:

IS THIS HEALTH, WEALTH, PERSONAL DEVELOPMENT, OR A RELATIONSHIP TOPIC? _____

TOPIC IDEA:

_____

TOPIC TITLE: How to _____ Without

_____

(add some numeric metric)_____.

Remember Total Alignment

The most effective webinars are where the topic, title, content, and offer are in complete alignment with what your audience wants. If you choose to include a blog post and content upgrade in your funnel, this blog post, and content upgrade must also be in complete alignment.

Know the **biggest** pain point or **desirable result** your **audience** wants

Create an **offer** that solves your audience biggest frustration/pain point or desirable result.

Create a **webinar topic** that gives people what they want as well as shows them why your offer is the logical next step.

Create a compelling **webinar title** that is result-oriented and promises your audience the result that they want.

Sign New Client

!

Note: When writing a **blog post** to attract an audience to your webinar, make sure the blog post is in alignment with your webinar topic. The blog post doesn't have to be the same as your webinar topic, but should support your topic and offer.

NOTES:

_____

_____

_____

_____

_____

_____

_____

_____

_____

Day 26
Breaking It Down - What Will Your Audience Learn?

On Day 26, you will be breaking down exactly what your audience will be learning. Why should they attend? Why even show up? Your response to these questions will be crucial to crafting your webinar and converting those webinar signups.

Using the previous potty training example, here's an example of the bullet points for the webinar topic: How To Potty Train Your Puppy In The Next Seven Days Without Having An Accident.

- How to teach your dog to hate going inside the house.
- The three simple steps to having your dog go in one spot outside all the time.
- The top 3 mistakes that new puppy owners teach to make their dog go inside the house and how to avoid them.
- How to teach your puppy to alert you when it's time to go outside.

EXERCISE

FINAL TOPIC TITLE:

WHAT WILL YOUR AUDIENCE LEARN?:

1.

2.

3.

4.

5.

NOTES:

_____

_____

_____

_____

_____

_____

_____

_____

_____

_____

NOTES:

_____

_____

_____

_____

_____

_____

_____

_____

_____

_____

_____

_____

_____

_____

Day 25
Creating the Visuals

It's everyone's favorite day - graphics and the visuals! It's best to get this out of the way! Once you have your official webinar title, you can go into graphic design software such as Photoshop, Canva.com, or RelayThat.com.

> **!**
>
> TIP: The best time, statistically, to host a webinar is 1:00 PM EST. This is going to depend on your audience, however. If you work a 9-5 or if your audience includes people that work a corporate job, 1:00 pm EST is not going to be the best time. You may have to host your webinars at night, 7:00 PM Eastern or 8:00 PM Eastern. Be mindful of dinner times, lunchtimes and weekends. Weekends are the least popular days for obvious reasons.

RESOURCES:

- **Canva:** https://www.canva.com/

- **Adobe Photoshop:**
  https://www.adobe.com/products/photoshop.html

- **RelayThat:** https://www.relaythat.com/

- **For a full list of resources go to:**
  https://www.aprillereed.com/bookresources/

NOTES:

NOTES:

_____

_____

_____

_____

_____

_____

_____

_____

_____

_____

_____

_____

_____

Day 24
Your Webinar Outline: Develop Your Intro

Your webinar outline is going to be your best friend during the next three weeks!

The outline will help you map out what you will be saying to your audience and teach them. Your webinar outline is vital to making sure you're giving value, and it will also help you ease into your offer and webinar funnel.

YOUR WEBINAR COMPRISES OF THREE PARTS:

1. **INTRO**

    - BUILD RAPPORT AND A CASE FOR YOUR WEBINAR
        - SHARE YOUR ORIGIN STORY

2. **TEACHING CONTENT**

    - INTRODUCE YOUR SYSTEM /METHOD/FRAMEWORK
    - DEBUNK THEIR INTERNAL FALSE BELIEFS
    - DEBUNK THEIR EXTERNAL FALSE BELIEFS

3. **OFFER**

    - CALL TO ACTION
    - TRIAL CLOSES
    - -Q & A

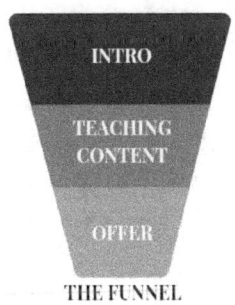

Think of your webinar like a funnel. Some people worry as attendees drop off, but this is expected and usually a good thing when conditions are right.

We want attendees to pre-qualify themselves so that those who see your offer are likely more serious about seeking help with their problem.

THE FUNNEL

Your introduction is the first part of the funnel where we build rapport and create a case for why they should attend the webinar and stay until the end.

EXERCISE:

INTRO

- BUILD RAPPORT AND BUILD A CASE:
    - Who is this webinar for, and who is it not for
    - Optional: What three mistakes are the making (Optional to include in your webinar, and it will add more time to the duration of your webinar.
    - Establish yourself as the expert/ give social proof

- YOUR ORIGIN STORY:
  Everyone has an origin story. Where were you, and what started you on this journey to find the solution to the problem you have now?

---

*For assistance with a webinar script and training videos to help with you begin you see sales with a 7-15 minute webinar version, check out the Webinar Jumpstart Toolkit self-study course: **www.aprillereed.com/bookresources/**

NOTES:

_____

_____

_____

_____

_____

_____

_____

_____

_____

_____

_____

_____

_____

Day 23
Your Webinar Outline: Develop Your Teaching Content

When creating your teaching content, do not have more than five teaching points. I love the rule of 3. So my webinars will typically have three teaching points.

THE FUNNEL

Below is the breakdown of how I structure the content that I want to teach on the webinar.

EXERCISE:

TEACHING CONTENT

- INTRODUCE YOUR SYSTEM/METHOD/BLUEPRINT
    - The first thing you will teach is your step-by-step system. Show your audience how your system works (your vehicle) and demonstrate it's the solution they've been looking for. Don't just tell them your system is good; show them.

- DEBUNK THEIR INTERNAL FALSE BELIEFS
    - Then teach how the system can work for them. Your audience will most likely have false internal beliefs, so you want to combat them here.

- DEBUNK THEIR EXTERNAL FALSE BELIEFS
    - Once they believe your system will work for them, you must address any external beliefs about them being able to implement your solution (i.e., not having an email list).

---

*For a video explaining this concept visit
www.aprillereed.com/bookresources/

NOTES:

_____

_____

_____

_____

_____

_____

_____

_____

_____

_____

_____

_____

_____

_____

Day 22
Your Webinar Outline: Develop Your Offer

Your offer is the most important, which is why we start with creating it first. What main result do your attendees or target market want to be solved? They are hungry for the solution. Please ensure the result that they want, your offer and your webinar topic and title are in total alignment, which you  should have had done in week 1. Now let's break this offer down into your webinar.

You can get a **FREE** copy of the book Expert Secrets Here: **www.aprillereed.com/pages/expertsecrets** or going to the resource page here: **www.aprillereed.com/bookresources/** It is a goldmine and will explain the following concept further.

EXERCISE:

OFFER
- CALL TO ACTION
    - Create The Stack of your offer. And the offer is a list of your products, or if you are sending people to a discovery call, you will still need to stack your offer and present them in an even more compelling way. Learn about The Stack on page 250 in the Expert Secrets book.

- TRIAL CLOSES
    - Sprinkle trial closes in the offer section of your webinar and throughout your entire webinar. Trial closes are easy yeses your audience can commit to. It's compared to the Pied Piper effect.

- Q&A
  - Be sure to add a Q&A at the end. Some people do 15 minutes, but I say to hold a Q&A for as long as people want to ask questions.

If you would like Canva product mockups for your offer and The Stack slides, you can purchase them here: **www.aprillereed.com/offergraphicskit/**

---

*For assistance with a webinar script and training videos to help with you begin you see sales with a 7-15 minute webinar, check out the Webinar Jumpstart Toolkit here: **www.aprillereed.com/bookresources/**

NOTES:

_____

_____

_____

_____

_____

_____

Day 21
Review and Catch Up Day

It's the final day of the week, and you're almost done! Yesterday's assignment was heavy, and you may need an extra day to make sure you have your ducks all in a row, so consider this catch-up day.

CHECKLIST:

☐ Choose what mega niche your product will fall under.

☐ If your offer does not easily fall under one of the mega niches, decide how to market your offer to fit in only ONE mega niche category.

☐ Decide on your offering.

☐ Choose your webinar day and time

☐ Choose your webinar software or be in the process of deciding

☐ Invest in a good external microphone. Your iPhone earbuds are good enough if need be.

☐ Decide what program will be delivering your email auto-responder

☐ What program will you use to create your landing pages (Registration page, Thank you page, Replay page, Sales page)

☐ Create your webinar topic and title

☐ Does your title have a numeric metric to make it POP?

- [ ] Create your 3-5 teaching points, so your audience will know what they will learn.

- [ ] Are your teaching points result-oriented or create curiosity?

- [ ] Design your (or outsource) Title page and repurpose it for social media

- [ ] Use design websites like:

  - **Canva:** www.canva.com/

  - **Photoshop:** www.adobe.com/

  - **RelayThat:** www.relaythat.com/

- [ ] Start creating your webinar outline. Remember Intro, Content, Offer.

- [ ] If you know who you will use to host your webinar, now is a good time to schedule it if you haven't already done so.

- [ ] Integrate and link your webinar software to your landing page builder. Sync your landing page builder to your email software.

- [ ] TEST! Test your signup process as if you were signing up for the webinar.

NOTES:

_____

_____

_____

NOTES:

_____

_____

_____

_____

_____

_____

_____

_____

_____

_____

_____

_____

NOTES:

WEEK 2

COUNTDOWN FROM DAYS 20 To 14

Day 20
Creating Your Registration Page

Create your registration page and link it to your webinar platform if needed.

EXERCISE:

TITLE:

DATE:

TIME:

BULLET POINTS:

_____

_____

_____

_____

_____

_____

!

TIP: Add a countdown on your page as it will promote urgency and encourage sign-ups.

NOTES:

_____

_____

_____

_____

_____

_____

_____

_____

_____

_____

_____

_____

_____

Day 19
Creating Your Thank You Page

Today, you will be creating a custom thank you page. Your attendees will see this page right after they sign up. Be creative with what they will see.

Some options include:

*A tripwire page (a small offer)

*Thank you page with your social media links

*Thank you page with share links if they'd like to share the webinar with their friends

*Thank you page with a link to your Facebook Page

*Thank you page with a video

EXERCISE:

THANK YOU PAGE COPY:

_____

_____

_____

_____

_____

_____

> **!**
>
> TIP: Clickfunnels is a great tool for a one-stop shop. You can start your free 14 day trial today.
>
> For all my recommendations of resources, tools and equipment go to **www.aprillereed.com/bookresources/**

NOTES:

_____

_____

_____

_____

_____

_____

_____

_____

_____

NOTES:

_____

_____

_____

_____

_____

_____

_____

_____

_____

_____

_____

_____

_____

_____

Day 18
Creating Your Email Confirmation

The confirmation email lets your attendees know they are registered for your webinar.

I love creating this email before any other email because this is the email that goes out first once someone signs up for your webinar. Once you have your pages (registration and thank you) and webinar software linked and in place, you technically can begin to get signups.

You may not choose to promote yet; however, you can share the link to some of your blog posts for early signups. Just make sure to test that you have everything hooked up correctly before doing so.

You will know everything is so-far-so-good when you register on your registration page and, after doing so, are immediately sent to the thank you page. You should also receive a confirmation email as well.

CONFIRMATION EMAIL CHECKLIST:

The confirmation email should have at minimum the following:

- [ ] Email subject
- [ ] Date and time of the webinar
- [ ] Link for the webinar
- [ ] Reminder to show up live
- [ ] Personality

You can add more information about the topic and what they will learn that day.

EXERCISE:

Write your confirmation email copy:

Email Subject Headline: Yahoo! You're confirmed.

Body:_____

_____

_____

_____

_____

_____

_____

Call To Action:

_____

Best Wishes,

Name

P.S._____

_____

NOTES:

_____

_____

_____

_____

_____

_____

_____

_____

_____

_____

_____

_____

_____

Day 17
Create a Webinar Replay Page
and Replay Email

It's up to you if you provide a replay after the webinar. A replay page is typically going to have information on the offer and recording of the webinar.

Create Your Replay Email

Send your replay email the day after your webinar with a link to the replay page and sales page. You can send this email to your entire list or only to those who attended the live webinar, even those who stayed for a few minutes.

In addition to your replay page directing people to your sales page, the replay email will also send people to the sales page.

The Replay Email is quick and easy. There's not much to say in this email. Write a short blurb inviting those who registered for the webinar to watch the replay, followed by an invite to the sales page.

NOTE: Invite them to the sales page and not the checkout page.

EXERCISE:

Write your replay email copy:

Email Subject Headline: Yahoo! You're confirmed.

Short Blurb: _____

_____

_____

_____

Invite to replay page: _____

_____

_____

Invite to Sales page: _____

_____

_____

_____

Best Wishes,
Your Name

NOTES:

_____

_____

_____

_____

_____

_____

_____

_____

_____

_____

_____

_____

_____

Day 16
Create a Sales Page and Checkout Page, or Button Sending Them to Your Calendar to Book

Today you'll want to make sure you have your funnel offer ready before the webinar is live!

Your link will depend on if you are selling them a program or a one-on-one offer. You can also send your attendees to a calendar to book a call with you.

CONFIRMATION PAGE:

Regardless of where you send them, be sure to create an order summary, the confirmation page of their order, or confirm the appointment they selected on your calendar.

The good news is that the confirmation page will most likely be third-party provided, so there's nothing you need to create. Just make sure the page is linked and working correctly so that once someone completes a sale or book on your calendar, they immediately see the confirmation page.

NOTES:

_____

_____

_____

_____

NOTES:

_____

_____

_____

_____

_____

_____

_____

_____

_____

_____

_____

_____

_____

Day 15
Create Webinar Invite Emails For Your List

Like the promotional graphics, these emails will go out to your entire list to remind them of the upcoming webinar.

You may want to use the promotional copy you have already created to repurpose your content. Use the exercise below to map out each email.

EXERCISE:

Email Subject

Headline:_____

_____

Body: _____

_____

_____

_____

_____

Call To Action:_____

_____

_____

Email Subject

Headline:_____

_____

Body: _____

_____

_____

_____

_____

_____

_____

_____

_____

Call To Action:_____

_____

NOTES:

Day 14
Create Email Reminders to Encourage Live Attendance

After the confirmation email, your audience should receive several emails before the webinar as a reminder. The goal is to get them to show up live.

EMAIL CHECKLIST:

Each email should have at minimum the following:

- ☐ Subject
- ☐ Date and Time
- ☐ Link for the webinar
- ☐ Reminder to show up live
- ☐ Personality

What emails to send:

Reminder emails

Confirmation email (send immediately after sign up - Created on day 17) Reminder email (send 2-3 days before the webinar and remind them to show up live.)

Tomorrow's The Day email (send the morning before the webinar)

Day of webinar emails

Early morning email
The hour before the email
15 minute before (or 10 minutes)
We're live email (At the start of webinar)

Email Subject

Headline:_____

_____

Body: _____

_____

_____

_____

_____

_____

_____

_____

_____

Call To Action:_____

_____

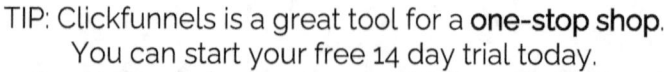

!

TIP: Clickfunnels is a great tool for a **one-stop shop**.
You can start your free 14 day trial today.

For recommendations of resources, tools, and
equipment to use, go to **www.aprillereed.com/
bookresources/**

NOTES:

_____

_____

_____

_____

_____

_____

_____

_____

WEEK 3

COUNTDOWN FROM DAYS 13 To 7

Day 13
Review and Catch Up Day:
Finalize Your Webinar Content and Emails

Consider this another catch-up day if you haven't yet finalized your webinar content. Remember: your outline may not be perfect.

Perfection may not come until you have had your webinar and get feedback and tweak your webinar based on the questions you receive. You're always going to be tweaking and testing your webinar!

CHECKLIST:

- ☐ Complete your webinar content.
- ☐ Create the registration page
- ☐ Create the thank you page
- ☐ Create the confirmation you're registered email
- ☐ Sign up yourself and make sure when you register that you are sent to the thank you page and receive the confirmation email
- ☐ Create the webinar replay page & replay email
- ☐ Create sales page and checkout page
- ☐ OPTIONAL: Instead of a checklist page, send people to your calendar to book a call with you for high ticket offers.
- ☐ Create Webinar Invite Emails For Your List
- ☐ Create Email Reminders To Encourage Live Attendance

NOTES:

_____

_____

_____

_____

_____

_____

_____

_____

_____

_____

_____

_____

_____

Day 12
Scheduling Your Promotional Graphics

Remember those graphics we created last week? Well, they're about to come in handy! Scheduling is key when it comes to this - you can use tools like Hootsuite, SocialBee, Smarterqueue, MeetEdgar, or Planoly for Instagram to schedule all your promotional content.

You'll want to schedule 6 days of promotional posts on your platform. If you use Instagram and Facebook, create similar posts for both platforms. Make this easy and repurpose copy from your promotional email to drive traffic to your webinar registration page.

CHECKLIST:

- [ ] Day 6 Post (Platform 1 _____)
- [ ] Day 6 Post (Platform 2 _____)
- [ ] Day 5 Post (Platform 1 _____)
- [ ] Day 5 Post (Platform 2 _____)
- [ ] Day 4 Post (Platform 1 _____)
- [ ] Day 4 Post (Platform 2 _____)
- [ ] Day 3 Post (Platform 1 _____)
- [ ] Day 3 Post (Platform 2 _____)
- [ ] Day 2 Post (Platform 1 _____)
- [ ] Day 2 Post (Platform 2 _____)
- [ ] Day 1 Post (Platform 1 _____)
- [ ] Day 1 Post (Platform 2 _____)
- [ ] Morning of webinar post (Platform 1 _____)
- [ ] Morning of webinar post (Platform 2 _____)

NOTES:

_____

_____

_____

_____

_____

_____

_____

_____

_____

_____

_____

_____

_____

Day 11
Create and Schedule Your Follow Up Emails

Oh, and you thought we were done with emails. Some people will need to think through it - that's where your follow-up emails come in!

Your post-webinar emails or follow-up emails announce the replay (already created previously), reminds them of your offer, and address common objections.

These emails are where you would add any fast action bonuses or timers for your offer.

Your live stream can be you addressing after-the-webinar questions and restating the offer. Or your live can be a case-study with a past client talking about their experience with your program. Instead of going live, you can also replace it with a case-study email.

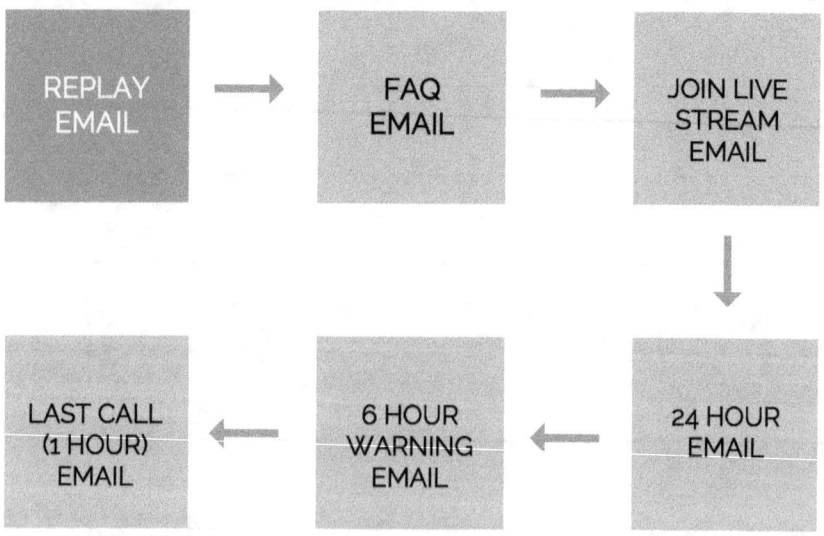

Make additional copies of this page if need be.

Email Subject Headline:_____

_____

Body: _____

_____

_____

_____

_____

_____

_____

_____

_____

_____

Call To Action:_____

_____

NOTES:

_____

_____

_____

_____

_____

_____

_____

_____

_____

_____

_____

_____

_____

Day 10
Practice Day

Let's sprinkle in an official practice day. Remember you'll want to practice your webinar about three times. This step is crucial to making sure your webinar goes as smoothly as possible before the big day.

CHECKLIST:

- ☐ Practice your webinar. This is a dress rehearsal.
- ☐ Have a friend or family attend the practice webinar to give you insight.
- ☐ Record this practice run and listen to it afterward for self-feedback.

> !
>
> TIP: You should be in PROMOTION mode! Change all call to actions on your website and social media to the webinar link.

Running Paid Traffic

At least 9-10 days leading to your webinar, start running Facebook ads if you plan to do so. Run to hot and warm traffic only.

It takes about 72 hours for your Facebook ads to optimize and understand your target audience and interests. So be patient before changing anything.

> !
>
> TIP: When running Facebook ads, start with warm traffic versus cold traffic. It will be cheaper and you can test your ad image and copy on a cheaper budget.

NOTES:

NOTES:

_____

_____

_____

_____

_____

_____

_____

_____

_____

_____

_____

_____

Day 9
Review and Catch Up Day

WOW! You've been moving along, and your reward is another review and catch-up day. Use this day to catch up on anything you need to finish.

Or skip ahead.

CHECKLIST:

- [ ] If you haven't done so yet, complete your webinar content.

- [ ] Now is the time to order any equipment you weren't able to purchase during the pre-planning days.

- [ ] Do you have the ability to wire into your webinar? No WiFi.

- [ ] Schedule your webinar promo posts six days out from your webinar.

- [ ] Continue working/ complete your post-webinar follow-up emails. (At least have your webinar replay page and replay email completely done and ready to go!!!!)

- [ ] Practice your webinar at least three times as if you were doing the real thing. Please, this is NOT optional. Webinarjam and GotoWebinar give you the ability to host a practice webinar.

- [ ] On day 10, run paid ads to warm and hot traffic. In my opinion, do not even bother with cold traffic for right now.

- [ ] If there are any previous tasks not mentioned here left undone, work on those and GET THEM DONE!!!!

- [ ] If you've enjoyed this workbook. Please leave a comment here: help@aprillereed.com

You can also submit a comment at
www.aprillereed.com/bookresources/

NOTES:

_____

_____

_____

_____

_____

_____

_____

_____

_____

_____

_____

_____

Day 8
Schedule 3-4 Facebook Lives/Videos

The next thing you want to do is schedule out two to three Facebook lives or recorded videos talking about the problem they are having and inviting them to your upcoming webinar. This is to get them excited, signed up, and ready for your fantastic knowledge!

Your first two Facebook lives acknowledge their pain. You talk about what the solution looks like and why it's essential to get their pain solved.

The next Facebook live or two should follow the same theme, but this time, you will direct them to sign up for your webinar. How long are these lives? We're talking about **10 minutes**.

Prefer YouTube or Instagram Live? **Go for it!**

The best way to come up with topics is to note what people ask you the most and make lives centered around those questions. If you're new and not getting any questions, search online, social media, Google, Reddit, and other places to see what questions are most popular with your niche.

TOPIC IDEAS EXAMPLES FOR VIRTUAL ASSISTANT SERVICES:

- When To Know Its The Best Time To Hire Your First VA.
- Top Mistakes Creatives Makes That Causes Overwhelm And Unfinished Tasks.
- The Top 10 Tasks To Outsource To A VA
- How To Know The Difference Between A Good VA And A Not-so Good VA The 3 Types Of VAs Your Should Have On Your Team
- How VAs Can Add 300 Minutes Back Into Your Day
- Case Study: How One Stay At Home Mom Earned $130K In 6 Months By Doing Less

Now it's Your turn...

Come up with 3 - 4 topics to live stream over the next few days.

Create a short blurb to post, so your followers will know you're going live tomorrow or about to go live in 15 minutes. Also, repurpose that post as an email and send it to your list.

①

②

③

④

NOTES:

_____

_____

_____

_____

_____

_____

_____

_____

_____

_____

_____

_____

_____

NOTES:

_____

_____

_____

_____

_____

_____

_____

_____

_____

_____

_____

_____

Day 7
Go Live on Facebook

Being present on social media a few days before the webinar is crucial to converting your organic reach. Using Facebook live or any other live streaming, you'll want to invite your audience to the webinar and talk about the topic for no more than 10-15 minutes.

Facebook Live Checklist

☐ Be in a quiet place. Hardwire with an Ethernet cable for live streaming. However, if you cannot, have a good WiFi connection.

☐ Have the webinar link ready to drop in the comments.

☐ Welcome viewers and replayers and Introduce yourself.

☐ Tell them the hook. Why should they listen?

☐ Engage the audience with a question.

☐ State the problem they are having.

☐ Deliver your three main points on the subject.

☐ Pitch the webinar with a link for them to sign up.

☐ Print out the Live Streaming Cheat Sheet on the next page and use it as a script for your next live stream.

LIVE STREAMING CHEAT SHEET

---

1. WELCOME EVERY ONE AND INTRODUCE YOURSELF

2. HOOK: STATE THE TOPIC AND WHY THEY SHOULD LISTEN

3. ENGAGE: ASK A QUESTION THAT REQUIRES A SIMPLE RESPONSE

4. STATE THE PROBLEM THEY ARE HAVING

5. DELIVER THE SOLUTION IN 3 EASY STEPS

6. GIVE A CALL TO ACTION.

NOTES:

WEEK 4

COUNTDOWN FROM DAYS 6 To 0

Day 6
Invite Your List

On Day 6, you'll want to send an email directly to your list about the webinar.

If you have already scheduled this email to go out, there is not much to do here.

The day before the webinar, you'll want to send another invite. Again, make it easy and schedule an email broadcast.

NOTES:

_____

_____

_____

_____

_____

_____

_____

_____

NOTES:

Day 5
Social Media: Invite Your Followers

On Day 6, you sent an email directly to your list about the webinar. The day before the webinar, you'll want to send a similar one.

Much like the previous day, you'll want to make good use of your current, organic audience by inviting them to the webinar.

Consider your different platforms: do you have a podcast? Or maybe an active Instagram?

Pinterest isn't social media, it is a search engine like YouTube, but none the less can you create content to share on these platforms as well?

Get creative with different platforms and promotions you can use to promote your webinar and get more people coming on live!

If you like, use the same script you used for your Facebook live.

NOTES:

_____

_____

_____

_____

NOTES:

Day 4
Complete Your Webinar Slides

By now, you should have the title slide and your offer designed. Today, you'll be creating the remaining design of your slides to add more visual elements to the webinar.

You're going to create seven to ten different graphics just to show a little variety in your PowerPoint and add your photos of yourself when you go through your story and some other graphics as well.

Remember: People are not there for your graphics. However, it always helps to have amazing graphics to give off a great first impression.

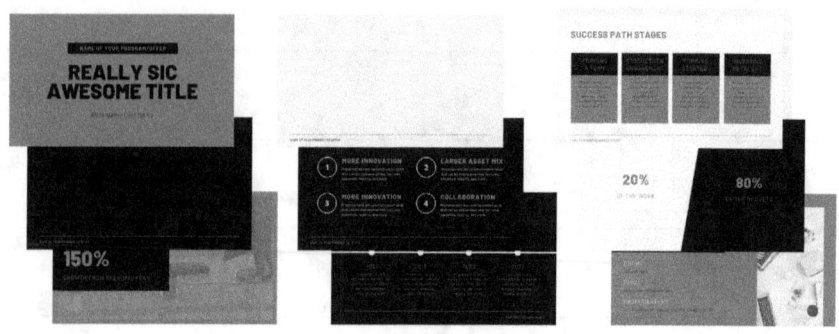

NOTES:

_____

_____

_____

NOTES:

_____

_____

_____

_____

_____

_____

_____

_____

_____

_____

_____

_____

_____

_____

Day 3
Practice, Practice, and Practice Again

Did you practice at least three times? Find places where you're going to stumble. Find places where it's not going to flow as well and is not going to make sense.

Remember: nobody is going to be as excited as you are. Be eager to be there, and your audience will match your excitement.

!

TIP: Find a friend or family member to listen to your webinar and give you feedback.

They won't be able to give you feedback on your offer if they're not your ideal customer, but they'll be able.

NOTES:

_____

_____

_____

_____

_____

NOTES:

Day 2
Review and Catch Up Day

It's time for a little review and R and R. And guess what? You're almost done! Use this day to go back through the material and catch up on anything overlooked, missed, or incomplete.

Below are the main things you want to make sure you have done:

RECAP CHECKLIST:

☐ You have created your offer, and it's in total alignment with your webinar topic and title.

☐ You have created the essential pages of your webinar funnel (Registration, Thank you, Replay, Sales Page, Confirmation Page)

☐ Your promotional graphics and posts are sending to promote webinar signups.

☐ You've signed up for your webinar and was directed to the thank you page, and received the confirmation emails.

☐ Your webinar presentation is done, and you have practiced it at least three times as if you were doing the real show to knock out as many kinks as possible.

NOTES:

_____

_____

_____

NOTES:

_____

_____

_____

_____

_____

_____

_____

_____

_____

_____

_____

_____

_____

Day 1
GET SOME REST!

Tomorrow is the BIG DAY!

Get some rest and stop stressing - there is no need to stress out now as you have done everything you can to promote this webinar and prepare for it.

If you must do more tweaking on your webinar slides, do so today and practice through it again. DO NOT touch your tomorrow. Tomorrow is just about getting your mental head in the game for a fantastic presentation.

NOTES:

_____

_____

_____

_____

_____

_____

_____

_____

NOTES:

Day 0
Day of Webinar

Today's the day! You're about to go live and wow your audience - and hopefully sell your program or offer! Today is all about delivering great content and testing your offer.

Here's a checklist for the day of your webinar:

- ☐ Make sure your desktop or laptop is hardwired to the internet using an Ethernet cable. **NO WIFI!**
- ☐ Turn off your ringer, remove your yapping dog, turn off notifications.
- ☐ Start your webinar at least 15 minutes early to address any last-minute problems.
- ☐ Remember to RECORD your webinar.

YOU ARE DONE!

Give yourself a high five because you did it, friend. But you're not done yet - here are your next to-dos after the webinar.

Day -1
After The Webinar (The Next Day)

- ☐ Change your webinar page to a WAITLIST for your next webinar or an opt-in for your newsletter. Do this manually or use a paid service like **Deadline Funnel** to direct traffic where you want them to go.
- ☐ Go LIVE on Facebook about the webinar you just did and answer any additional questions. This is an excellent opportunity for more exposure.

Evaluating the Webinar

When you're just starting, do webinars live and get that instant feedback to make your webinar the best-recorded webinar it can be.

Maybe the thought of hosting a webinar live freaks you out, but the truth of the matter is that if your webinar is not making money live, it's not going to be making money recorded either.

So we start with live webinars, and when you've done a few live launches and you are happy with your results, such as your conversions, then you can move into automated webinars.

You'll love the instant feedback you'll receive on a live webinar launch because you're able to move and shift where needed. You're able to test on the spot.

Testing, tweaking and improving, and you'll be able to gauge the audience's engagement with your material. And as you get questions, you can add them in your very next presentation.

There's nothing better than being completely confident that your automated webinar WILL pull in the revenue you want it to month after month, week after week. Your content will get better and your message stronger.

But you're just hoping it's a winner when you do one live webinar and move straight to automated or bypass live and go prerecorded from the jump. Do multiple lives during your launches until you are at this confidently.

So how many live webinars do YOU have to do? As many as it takes... and don't compare. Someone may only need to do four live webinars, while someone else may need to do 16.

There's no magic number. But if you want to challenge yourself and ensure the best darn webinar 'eva' - try doing one or two live webinars every month for a year......OK, OK, I DON'T want to scare you... we'll just start with doing four live ones in a single launch.

Once you're satisfied, move onto automated. That's where we all want to go.

CHECKLIST:

- [ ] Watch your replay. Take note of where you could improve and also what you ROCKED!
- [ ] Survey the webinar attendees - you can do this by writing a short email to the webinar attendees and sending them a form or just asking for email feedback.
- [ ] Determine your next webinar date!
- [ ] Continue to evaluate and work towards the perfection you are trying to achieve.

!

TIP: Once you have a fully converting and awesome webinar, you'll want to automate it to generate passive income for your offer.

NOTES:

NOTES:

_____

_____

_____

_____

_____

_____

_____

_____

_____

_____

_____

_____

_____

SHOW ME
THE MONEY

6 FIGURE BUSINESS PLAN

$5000 offer x 20 CLIENTS = $100,000

Listen to the episode above where I explain the 6 figure business plan: **https://www.aprillereed.com/ bookresources**

"You just got to love people when working one-on-one, or you will get burnt out." [07:58]

"If working with you is what they want to do, you can coach people into saying yes to investing in themselves and yes to their future." [14:34]

Are you ready to make six-figures this year? Whether you are a coach or a consultant, this episode is for you. I will tell you two strategies to help you get to that six figures, so pay attention and don't miss out!

In this episode, you will learn:

- What Strategy #1 is
- The purpose of a strategy session
- What happens if you sell your coaching on a per session basis
- What Strategy #2 is
- Why this strategy works

6 FIGURE BUSINESS MODEL

  Free content & freebie
to grow your email list

$: 27-47 (Can price at
$147 or $197 and include
offers and discounts.)

1-hour audio with a
workbook. 1-hour
video with a
workbook. Ebook.
Planner. Swipe file.
Template. Audio/
Video/ Transcription.
mini-course.

$$: $500 - $2,000

Signature Course

$$$: Monthly recurring
revenue, $20 - $97 per
month, or a high-end like
mastermind charging
$500+ per month.

A membership site
for recurring revenue
or coaching.

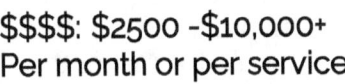

$$$$: $2500 -$10,000+
Per month or per service.

High-end coaching.
One-on-one private
coaching. High-end
group coaching.
High-end
mastermind.

MILLIONAIRE MINDSET BREAKTHROUGH

I will keep this short, and it's the fact that **a million dollars** are not as hard to obtain as you may think.

I didn't say it was easy. I didn't say it wouldn't require work. But what I am saying is that a **$1,000,000** is **NOT** as hard to obtain as you may think.

Look at the basic math below and let your mind wander on the possibilities:

Webinar selling High-ticket item:

You need **100 people** to buy your $10,000 item
You need **200 people** to buy your $5,000 item

Webinar selling a course:

You need **5,076 people** to buy your **$197 course**
You need **2,012 people** to buy your **$497 course**
You need **1,003 people** to buy your **$997 course**
You need **501 people** to buy your **$1997 course**

Webinar selling a membership:

You need **4200 members** paying **$20** per month for 12 months
You need **1,800 members** paying **$47** per month for 12 months
You need **900 members** paying **$97** per month for 12 months
You need **500 members** paying **$167** per month for 12 months
You need **300 members** paying **$278** per month for 12 months

$1,000,000

NOTES:

_____

_____

_____

_____

_____

_____

_____

_____

_____

_____

_____

_____

NOTES:

_____

_____

_____

_____

_____

_____

_____

_____

_____

_____

_____

_____

_____

WHAT THE TECH?!

RECOMMENDATIONS

DISCLAIMER: THESE ARE AMAZON.COM PRODUCTS AND PRICES MAY INCREASE OR DECREASE ANY TIME. FOR THIS LIST AND TO PURCHASE GO TO **WWW.APRILLEREED.COM/BOOKRESOURCES/**

MICROPHONES:

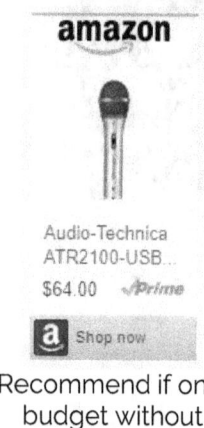

Audio-Technica ATR2100-USB...
$64.00 ✓Prime

Recommend if on a budget without compromising quality.

Blue Snowball USB...
$65.83 ✓Prime

Another quality microphone. Comes with stand.

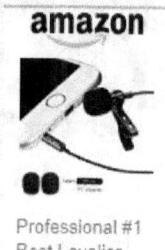

Professional #1 Best Lavalier...
$12.99 ✓Prime

Good sound and attaches to your iPhone (need an adapter for iPhone X and above. I use this for FB lives & YouTube.

BUNDLES: MIC, POP FILTER, HEADPHONES:

Audio Technica ATR2100-USB...
$89.00

Blue Microphone Yeti USB...
$139.99 ✓Prime

Blue Microphones...
$149.00

The first mic and bundle I purchased in my biz. I currently use.

POP FILTERS SHIELD THE MIC FOR SPIT AND DECREASE AIR BLASTS FROM USING WORDS THAT START WITH "B" OR "P" AND HISSING FROM FROM "S"

POP FILTERS:

If you purchased the Blue Yeti Bundles on page 102, you do not need to buy another pop filter.

| For any Microphone | For Blue Yeti Microphone | For ATR Microphone |

MICROPHONE STANDS:

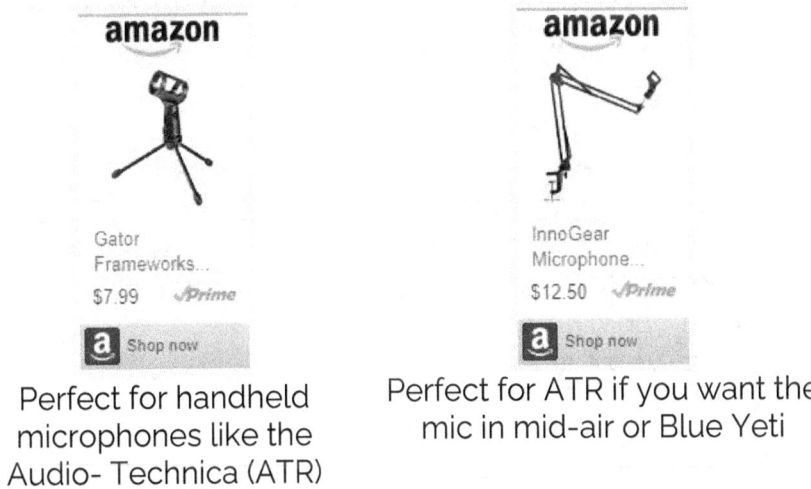

Perfect for handheld microphones like the Audio- Technica (ATR) Microphone

Perfect for ATR if you want the mic in mid-air or Blue Yeti

HEADPHONES:

You can easily just use your iPhone headphones.

WEBCAMS:

This is the **Logitech C920**
(I use this item for all my videos
when I'm not using my iPhone.)

Logitech C922
(A step up from Logitech C920.
However, according to Amazon
reviews, there's not a huge
difference.
Read reviews for yourself before
upgrading if you already have
C920)

WEBINAR PLATFORMS:

- Zoom (paid version) or Zoom Webinar*
- Demio*
- Easy Webinar
- Ever Webinar (Best for evergreen webinars/funnels)
- Webinar Ninja
- Stealth Seminars
- GoTo Webinar (Most reliable option)*
- Crowdcast
- YouTube Live/Hangout on Air (Free but less reliable)

PAYMENT PROCESSING:

- PayPal
- PayPal.Me
- Stripe
- Samcart
- Authorize.NET (If you want a merchant account.)

RESOURCES & TOOLS

I hope you enjoy this resource and tools section I've put together to help you rock your webinars. Most of the resources listed I have or currently using myself. Deciding on what tools and programs to use can be a headache, so this will save you a lot of time AND provides a list to make sure you're always using the best tools for your webinars, depending on your goals.

Google Drive:

Can you believe my 10-year-old introduced me to Google Drive LOL? Google Drive is great for creating content like your webinar script or saving files across the internet. You can also share files with others and manipulate the content in real-time without the burden of re-uploading a file like MS Word or Dropbox.

Evernote:

Evernote is great for brainstorming. My blog topics are stored here. I just love the app as well. I can take a picture with my phone and upload it right into Evernote. I also take pics of receipts. Evernote does a lot more as well. Click here for a great article on how to use Evernote for maximum results.

Dropbox:

I use Dropbox daily. I love how it syncs with all my computers. I use Dropbox mostly to store files, photoshoots, link my podcast episodes, and practically everything. You're able to share files and folders but not manipulate and auto-save like Google Drive. So think about that when deciding which files to save in Dropbox or Google Drive.

Microsoft PowerPoint:

Most people are familiar with Microsoft PowerPoint. Whether at your corporate job, in school, or as an entrepreneur, this is my go-to for the webinar presentation. PowerPoint is reliable, comes with many tools, and is easy to use if you're familiar with Word.

Keynote:

Keynote is just like PowerPoint but for Mac users. When making the presentation for clients, if they prefer Keynote, I usually create it in PowerPoint (because I'm more familiar) and convert it into Keynote, and it works just fine.

Google Slides:

You can create your webinar presentation using Google Slides. You're able to create and edit with your team in real-time easily. Google Slides is also free and can be used anywhere with an internet connection or download for use offline. Google Slides, like PowerPoint, comes with presentation themes, so you do not have to start from scratch.

Leadpages:

First off, I love Leadpages!!! I no longer use it because the extra expense made no sense with having Clickfunnels. Leadpages allow you to create all your webinar pages, sale pages, and more with the option to manipulate your colors, branding, images, and copy.

Canva 2.0:

I use Canva daily. 95% of my designs are created with Canva Pro. Canva comes with templates, stock images (free and paid), and the ability to upload your branding. Drawback: your images 'sometimes' come out blurry :(Get it together, Canva. But there's a workaround. Watch the video at **www.aprillereed.com/ bookresources/**

Photoshop CC:

What I can't do in Canva, I can do in Photoshop. You will not have any issues with blurriness in Photoshop, but there is a learning curve. If you're not familiar with this application, outsource or use Canva.

Upwork:

Upwork, like Fiverr, is a hub to find virtual assistants, copywriters, designers, and more. They make it easy to send out jobs and find the perfect freelancer for your project. They also have a Work Diary where you can see what your freelancer is working on. Payment for work is collected on Mondays.

Online Jobs | PH:

https://www.onlinejobs.ph. I have yet to use it personally, but I have a friend who has gotten great results. These freelancers are from the Philippines and offer virtual assistant work. There is a monthly fee for as long as you need to find "the one."

ClickFunnels:

ClickFunnels, in my opinion, is the king of funnels. At $97 per month, there's so many application you can get rid of to run your business. Here is where you can create your entire webinar funnel.

Zoom Webinar:

Zoom is what I use most times for video and webinars. At around $15, you can host your very own webinar that requires some manual labor on your part. They also have Zoom Webinar for an additional $40 per month. This will allow people to have a unique webinar link, and you can also use it to go live on Facebook and share your screen.

Go To Webinar:

Why do all the great things have to be so darn expensive? So this is the most **reliable** webinar platform I've encountered. The drawback is the need for Citrix, and it's **costly**. However, it is the leader in webinar deliverability. You can host up to 1000 attendees, and it won't crack.

Facebook Live:

Facebook continues to roll out more and more. You can go live on Facebook and show your screen. This means you can host a webinar for free. Bring up your PowerPoint presentation and go live in front of your registrants.

EverWebinar:

Even though Easy Webinar can host live, automated, and hybrid webinars and telesummits, I am listing it here for evergreen webinars only. There are far better options, in my opinion, for hosting a live webinar or a launch. Don't worry about this until you host your webinar live several times and have perfected it.

Aprille, webinars are cool and all. No, really, I get how powerful they are, but the thing only thing is I don't feel like creating PowerPoint slides, and I DO NOT want to be on camera. What can I do?

ANSWER: If you're not quite ready for webinars, you can get the same results with telesummits or teleseminars.

Instant Teleseminar:

Just like a webinar but NOT. I've never used Instant Teleseminar for my business, but it's mentioned and used by a lot of big names. There can be thousands of people on the call, and you're free to look at your notes. Hmmm, why haven't I tried this yet?!!! Let's face it; I just love webinars. But again, this is an excellent option if you want to host a call where no one can see you sweat or in sweatpants.

*Bonjoro:

I love Bonjoro and so do my customers. Bonjoro lets you send personalized welcome or thank-you videos to your customers. Anytime someone opts in or purchases, I get a message from Bonjoro, and I can send them a quick thank you video via email. And it's so much fun!!!!

ConverKit:

This what I use! Many big names use ConvertKit, like Pat Flynn and Nicole Walters, so why shouldn't I. Convertkit has the ability to build powerful automation like Infusionsoft without all the tech confusion. This is a powerful email marketing provider.

Aweber:

Aweber is a good option as well. They have added new features since I've last used them. It comes with a **30-day trial** and, like ConvertKit, can connect to RSS feeds if you have a podcast you like to email out to your subscribers.

Mailchimp:

Advantages of using Mailchimp are that it's free for up to 2,000 subscribers, and many platforms will easily integrate with Mailchimp. You may also find that many high-end courses will provide email tech video tutorials, with this service being one example.

Manychat (Messenger Bot):

Email marketing should be your best friend, but messenger bots should be your next best friend. Not everyone opens their email. Using this strategy in addition to email marketing is powerful. But one thing at a time. Manychat has a **free** version at the time of this writing.

Motionmail:

How about a **free** countdown timer for your offers right there in your email? Motionmail provides an excellent solution for this, especially if you're just starting out and cannot invest in something like Deadline Funnel.

Deadline Funnel:

No free option, but there is a **trial period**. Deadline Funnel is a timer and perfect for evergreen promotion. If you're ready for a timer or program that is a little more robust, try this.

Calendly:

Calendly offers a **free** calendar and very easy to use. When I first started, I used Calendly. However, I have moved on to AcuityScheduling, which is my recommendation. But Calendly is good too, so I'm listing it here.

AcuityScheduling:

If you're willing to pay $15 per month and have the option to send out nurturing emails, get paid before people can book on your calendar, sync to Google calendar, and a whole lot more, start here. They also have a free version, but this baby is worth the investment.

FOR A LIST OF THESE RESOURCES, PLEASE GO TO
WWW.APRILLEREED.COM/BOOKRESOURCES/

NEED ADDITIONAL HELP WITH YOUR FIRST OR NEXT WEBINAR?

Is The Webinar Club right for you?

Let's answer that question and help you find the answer.

I've put together a fun quiz. It's quick: You're ready for The Webinar Club if you...

> Are ready to follow a simple plan to get high-paying clients consistently month after month,

> Can dedicate 45-90 minutes a week to meeting your goal,

> Don't have time to waste on things that don't work anymore,

> Realize your current path isn't getting the results you're after,

> Want easy-to-follow guidance from someone who knows EXACTLY what you need.

If you're nodding and saying, "yes! YES!" to that pop quiz, you've just answered your big question.

So here's the next question...

Are you ready to join me?

YES! Then go to www.aprillereed.com/thewebinarclub

NOTES:

_____

_____

_____

_____

_____

_____

_____

_____

_____

_____

_____

_____

_____

NOTES:

NOTES:

NOTES:

NOTES:

NOTES:

NOTES:

NOTES:

_____

_____

_____

_____

_____

_____

_____

_____

_____

_____

_____

_____

_____

DOODLE NOTES:

DOODLE NOTES:

DOODLE NOTES:

DOODLE NOTES:

DOODLE NOTES:

DOODLE NOTES:

DOODLE NOTES: